Dedication

To all of us out here doing the work
of still figuring it all out.

YOUR (ALIGNED) GIRL IN A CRISIS

A PRACTICE IN NOT BORROWING TROUBLE

CINDY URBANSKI

Your Aligned Girl in a Crisis: A Practice in Not Borrowing Trouble
Cindy Urbanski

Published by Synergy Publishing Group, Belmont, NC
Cover illustration and design by KC Roberge
Formatting by Melisa Graham

Softcover, March 2026, ISBN 978-1-960892-64-5
Ebook, March 2026, ISBN 978-1-960892-65-2

CONTENTS

*Courage allows the successful woman to fail
and learn powerful lessons from the failure.
So that in the end, she didn't fail at all.*
—Maya Angelou

INTRODUCTION:
DON'T BORROW TROUBLE

"Don't borrow trouble" are the words with which I was raised. My grandmother spoke those words often. Over and over, in fact, to me. I was a child with a big imagination for all the "awful" that "might" happen. Until I was married, I lay awake most nights dreading the "awful." My husband, Bret, does an excellent impression of a weighted blanket, and that dealt with a lot of what I now know was deep anxiety and catastrophizing. (Thank you, over a decade of therapy!) Now, as a fifty-plus-year-old woman who has found some peace (most of the time, it's definitely a practice), I know my grandmother was telling me to release the outcome.

That is exceptionally challenging for my type A self. I can distinctly remember being five-years-old and having plans A, B, C, and so forth lined up to ensure that the outcome I wanted happened. It served me at times. I'll be the first to admit that once I set my mind to something, it is rare for me to fail. Yes, I am quite good at working all the systems to get what I want for myself and my people. And work I do. In fact, it can be said that I get worked up, into a frenzy! And here's the dirty secret: For a long time, if I couldn't ensure success, I did not try.

Case in point, I have a PhD without ever having taken statistics. Math is a struggle for me. I am embarrassed to admit that I went to my department chair and cried in her office until she found a way around the requirement for me. Had she not, I would have dropped out of the program and told myself I didn't need the stinking degree anyway! See, it's not as great as it sounds at first. I have countless stories like this. I did not have Maya Angelou's brand of courage.

As I learned to "just try," rather than guaranteeing the outcome, amazing things that my calculating mind never dreamed of started opening up. I started to take risks. I did things that I wasn't naturally good at doing. I embarked on areas of study where I didn't already know the answers. I tried and failed. And I actually learned. I let others take over in places where I needed help instead of doggedly holding on because I had to be sure of the outcome.

I didn't die!

And before, I was certain that I would.

Instead, trying those new things lit me up in ways I'd never before imagined, all because I could say, "I'm in my integrity to try this thing, and whatever happens, that will be okay because I am doing what I know is correct. That 'correct' action is all that matters." Or I can say, "This is not my wheelhouse, but it is yours, so I'm going to let go of the reins and trust. The outcome will be what it will be. And if it all burns down, we'll gain some wisdom!"

Because here's the secret I was missing: We have no control over the outcome. I can't ensure excellent test grades from my kids, but I can support them steadily and calmly and build courageous humans who can get out there, give it their all, and show people what they know. I can't stop cancer, and I can do all the things to catch it early and give me and mine the best chance of beating it.

And it's not about throwing one's hands up in the air and "letting go." That's tapping out and leaving a mess for someone else to clean up. Some things are worth holding on to and make us who we are.

This book is composed of essays and poems about learning to stop borrowing trouble and surviving the process.

Enjoy the journey!

XO,
Cindy

PRACTICING WHAT I PREACH (IS HARD!)

"I failed my test! I am mortified!" This was the message I sent to my closest friends after receiving a "fail" report on a standardized test to receive ICF (International Coach Federation).

It wasn't the end of the world. I was already a Body Mind Certified Coach©. I had been actively coaching for three years. This was just further certification for what I was already doing.

I could take it again in fourteen days, and to my knowledge, other than scoring in the 7th percentile in fourth grade on the spelling portion of the California Achievement Test, I've never failed a test in my life. To be fair, the California Achievement Test was not something a person could study for, and I was in the 99th percentile in all other subjects, which we now know points to a learning disability. Yes, I have a PhD in Urban Literacy, have worked with writers, and been a writer for thirty years, and I cannot spell worth a lick.

But I digress. This was a test for which I could study. No spelling was required. I did not pass it. Hard stop.

I also did not really study.

I took a practice test and scored 96 percent.

I felt I understood the material.

I looked at my list of priorities and the value of my time.

I decided that studying would be a waste of time.

I felt totally in my integrity when I chose not to study.

I rolled the dice.

I failed.

It took my breath away, and it was a growth edge all at the same time.

You see, for my whole life I have over-prepared for every test I've ever taken. I've been "ready" without a shadow of a doubt for two days before each test was to take place and spent the last two days reviewing. I white-knuckled the outcome.

And worse, if I didn't feel I was going to *be* ready, I didn't take the test.

I dropped trigonometry three times in undergrad before I finally audited it the third time and took it the fourth.

I fell in love with an upper-level Russian history course, also as an undergrad, and dropped it because all the material was so new to me I only scored a C+ on the first test.

I was white-knuckling my GPA and the outcome.

I left no room for failure and in-so-doing, cheated myself out of growth. I really loved Russian history.

This time, with this test, I may have received a "fail," and, yep, I have to come off the hip for a hundred dollars to take it again (which extra stings), and after I got over myself and looked again at Maya Angelou's words about failure that open this book, I didn't fail at all.

I stand by my choice not to waste precious time studying when I felt confident and my practice test grade was a 96. Now, I know that the practice test is not a reflection of the actual test. I will resist launching into a rant about standardized testing here because that will pull us away from the point. As my father-in-law often said, "It is what it is."

I know this test is no reflection of me as a coach. In fact, the day before and the day after this very test, I coached amazing women who were over the moon about my coaching skills. I felt solid in my power as a coach who empowers others. I felt in my soul that this test did not define me.

I spent a morning hunting down standardized study materials and made myself a study plan. That is the next correct step. Does that guarantee a pass the next time? Nope.

The old me would just say, "I don't need this certification," and rail against the systemic issues of standardized testing.

I'm trying something new. I'll do the next correct thing and see what happens.

Everything in me wants to go into assuring the outcome. And I'm resisting and allowing the chance to fail again so I can learn something.

Terrifying!

CHICANERY

When Mason, my last child, took off for college, after Mackenzie, my first child, got married and added a third grown child, Rahul, my son-in-love, to my brood, I started writing this book about releasing the outcome.

Why?

Well . . .

1) Nothing will test your inner control freak like having adult children.

2) I had begun to practice outcome releasing and felt a deep, deep shift in my anxiety level, my stress, and my soul. I wanted to share that story with anyone who would listen.

Now, I'm not suggesting that we throw our hands in the air and "let it all go" or stop working to solve problems.

I'm suggesting that when we analyze a problem and take what we believe are correct steps to solve it, without a death-grip on the outcome, it's plenty.

I'm suggesting we recognize what we can control and what we cannot.

The outcome is something we don't get to control.

And that's scary (at least for me) to recognize.

That said, I've had a lot of support to get to a place of peace around outcomes, and I still don't have it down. There are days when my death-grip returns and everything goes sideways.

And that's when I have to remind myself to reach for support.

- I have a coach and can reach out to her on Voxer whenever I need, or I can schedule a call that works with our schedules.
- I use writing, yoga, and walking to ground myself each morning.
- I talk with my trusted people.

And that's where the shifts happen that right the sinking ship.

For example: I was sitting in my sister-in-law's kitchen chatting about who knows what when my phone blinked. It was my college freshman son at 7:15 on a Saturday morning. My senses were on high alert before I even read the message . . .

"Are you awake? I need you," he wrote.

"Yes! Call at will," I replied.

I was twelve hours away from him with no airport nearby when I got this message.

He called. He calmly and carefully explained that his roommate had been sending him death threats and threats to his own life since 2 a.m. My son had talked to his sister and her husband in the night, who had advised him to stay out of the room and tell his intoxicated roommate to go to sleep. He had silenced his phone and complied. When he woke up, there were over three hundred more messages.

And now, in the light of day, he had walked back across campus without contacts or glasses and found that his roommate had barricaded the door.

Hence his call.

"Please don't let this kid be dead," was all I could think.

I matched my son's calm, assertive energy and told him to find help. I stayed on the phone while he knocked on doors and texted all four RAs in the building to no avail. We figured out how to call the emergency on-call resident assistant. She told him to call 911, and she was on her way.

The police came. They opened the door. My son made a statement and screenshotted the texts for the police and the campus welfare folks.

My son read them all to me. I was sick. They were equal parts terrifying and horrible. The kid went straight to my son's soft spots and landed the punches right in the gut.

I wanted to get in the car and head back south. I was supposed to drive five more hours north to a ninetieth birthday party. The police and campus were involved. My husband and I drove north as we spoke with our son and a campus well-being official. They reassured us that they would move my son to another room and look after him. Both my son and the adult sounded completely in control of the whole situation. I kept heading to the party with the idea that an airport was right where I was headed.

An hour later, my son and a good friend FaceTimed us from my son's room. They were speed-packing all of his stuff and getting it into the common area. They were hysterically funny, and shirtless.

"We have this, Mom!"

"Gentlemen, why are you naked?"

"We have pants, underwear, socks, and Jesus."

Jackson, my son's great friend, reassured me he had my son's back and that he would not leave his side. I exhaled. They were ridiculous and absolutely fine.

In the end, the roommate came back that afternoon, and my son spent the weekend unhoused. He slept on his friend's sofa, and several other friends made sure he was fed. Eventually he got to move, with the help of his friends, across campus. The university dropped the ball on helping my son and his deeply disturbed roommate.

We made it to campus the following Tuesday after making the party and all of our planned East Coast stops. I marched myself into the Office of Well-Being and calmly made them aware of the dropped balls, while my husband took my son to a baseball game. Things got sorted. Restraining orders were signed. The official things got done.

But that's not the point.

Until that moment, I would have been back on that campus by Saturday afternoon, whisking my son to an Airbnb and moving his stuff into his new room once it was available. But I released control just a little bit. *We* did, both his father and me. And my son grew because of this whole horrifying experience.

He knew I would get to him if he needed me, and he didn't need me.

He had his own big brain and the brains of his friends. The adults in the room didn't do their jobs, a theme in his life, and he didn't need them after the first genuine crisis was solved. He had good friends and his parents' support. He could depend on himself and his friends and make it.

I grew. My children are now young adults. They still need my guidance and support, but I don't need to swoop quite as fast and as deep. I forget this, and need reminding, but it doesn't make it any less true.

When the chicanery hits the fan, they have it.

My job is to hold the space for them to have it.

ALIGNED SWOOPING: A PRACTICE

Help is the sunny side of control
—Ann Lamott

I didn't swoop, and it turned out great for my son.
And at the same time, I carry and have carried
the title "your girl in a crisis" for most of my life.
I specialize in swooping into crisis situations and
helping where help is needed. I think I am excellent
at discerning the needs of those who are too
overwhelmed to name them and/or have too many
gremlins to ask. And then, I can make what is needed
happen. I am the most excellent of space holders.

[Enter record screeching]

I am a serial helper. And I'm starting to recognize
that sometimes it borders on mind reading . . .

"I'll hold space for that"
    For you
    For this thing we are manifesting
    For grief

For joy
For fear
For everything
Almost

I'll get right down beside you
In the muck
And sit.

I might pat your back
Or hold your hand
Or offer a gentle kiss on the forehead

I do it ALL.THE.TIME.
For ALL.THE.PEOPLE.

For real.

I hold space for the mama I don't know
in the checkout line
With a basket of groceries
and three screaming toddlers.

And don't get me started
On the strangers on the airplane
Whom my introverted self
Would prefer to ignore.

SO

WHY is it so HARD to sit
And hold space
For my husband?

The love of my life
My truest partner
My best friend?

Is it because we've spent 30 years solving problems
Together
And
I *think* I know where he is going in his mind
LONG before he does?

Is it simple impatience?

I know that when we work together
there is no problem
that we can't sort.

(Yes, I just threw that gauntlet at the feet of
the universe.)

So

WHY am I so fidgety when the man is working
his process?

WHY am I not holding space
Breathing quietly
Patiently?

Contrary to what I may think
I am no mind reader.

As you can see, I have studied and practiced and
made progress on this concept of actually holding

space versus swooping and controlling. I had this whole essay on "Aligned Swooping" written and was putting the finishing touches on this book when Mason messaged me in the year following the events of the "Chicanery" essay and all of its lessons. This time he was awash with sadness. I swooped and swooped hard.

The plan had been to go to Virginia the following evening and take him to an Airbnb post football game. We were going to spend the night and all day Sunday together, and I was going to return him to his 8 a.m. class on Monday before heading home. It was a solid plan.

I had a full day on my calendar. Bret, my husband, was out of town. It was Halloween, so I had plans to sit on my porch and enjoy handing out candy to our adorable neighborhood children. Also, I had cooked a week's worth of food for some clients who were coming to our magical retreat house and planned to drop that by on my way to the boy the following day. I had two very full days before our agreed-upon 8 p.m. pickup time.

I can't tell you exactly what happened except I panicked and my "control the outcome and control it NOW" kicked into high gear, and I began full-on swoopage. I wanted to "help." I ignored the fact that Mason had friends and mentors who were helping him. I ignored that he had ridden the wave of emotion rather than attempting to escape it. I ignored that he told me about it and said, "I am okay!"

I messaged the Airbnb to see if they were open a night early. I started plotting to fight Friday afternoon traffic out of Charlotte adding at least an hour of high-stress driving to my trip, stopping by the retreat house to leave the food, and then continuing to campus to pick up my child . . . *on Halloween*!

Now, if you've ever been a college student on Halloween, you know it is most certainly *not* helpful to have your mom show up and whisk you away.

Thankfully, I communicated my "helpful" plan to my husband, Bret, who kindly told me to stand down. My daughter, Mackenzie, gently told me the same when I told her I "might" go. Both checked in with Mason and reassured me he was A-okay and waiting 'til post-game the next night was correct. I checked in with Mason myself, and he said, "I promise I'll let you know if I need you," early in the day and then later, "I'll see you at 8 p.m. tomorrow."

All signs pointed to "stay." But my swooping ways pulled hard towards "GO!" I stayed, albeit tearfully and with tremendous anxiety.

And then, on the drive the next day, the universe handed me the Anne Lamott quote at the beginning of this piece through Brene Brown's *Dare to Lead* podcast that a great friend, who knows my swooping ways and will call me out on them, recommended.

I felt seen.

I felt called out.

I felt called up!

As I said, I had this essay in the bag. And my beta reader said it needed a story. I had one written that paints me in a much less controlling light. That story is true. And when I get triggered, I still want to swoop. Alas, even after two years of work on this book project, releasing the outcome is still hard when things are "important."

So here's the rest of the essay with which this story belongs.

Lately I have learned that in my swooping, I am a big ole enabler for many people I love. In my swooping, I actually take away power. That particular a-ha was deeply upsetting given my modus operandi is to empower people.

So this disempowerment had me in a hard conversation with my coach. I was bitter as all get out because I was exhausted from swooping and felt like I was being manipulated. In reality, I was turning myself wrong-side-out, reading minds left and right, and doing a whole lot of bossing a job that was not mine to boss.

I had a great example to follow that I was not following.

You see, my sainted mother-in-law was not afraid to call people out on their nonsense. She loved her people deeply, and she simply refused to enable them. She was the same with me. She believed in me and my power, and I rose to the occasion. Again and again.

This same woman would throw a sign on her tailor shop door that simply read "not here," hop in the car,

and drive to North Carolina from New York at any
sign of distress from Bret and me. She would then
proceed to dig us out from under the overwhelming
laundry and handle business, all the while letting us
know that we totally had it.

It was a gift.

It was aligned swooping.

She would come *when we asked for what
we needed!*

Aligned swooping is about two things: boundaries
and consent.

Boundaries: I have to hold boundaries for myself.

1) If you want my help, you need to ask for it. I'm
   going to trust you to tell me what you need!
2) If you ask for help and ignore my advice,
   that's on you. I will gather the facts and
   present them carefully as many times as you
   ask, and you still get to make your own choice.
   I will not beg you to do the thing.
3) I'm not going to repeatedly insert myself into
   your business. I repeat: I trust you to tell me
   what you need.

Consent:

1) If I see a need, I will ask, "What would feel
   supportive," rather than, "What can I do
   for you?"
2) If I have an idea, I'll ask you if you'd like to
   hear it.
3) If you say you have it, I will believe you!

This aligned swooping that was modeled for me
so well by my mother-in-law has been life-changing

for me and those I love. Yes, they are becoming more empowered, and they are learning the blessing of actually asking for what they need. As for me, I am right-side-out. My central nervous system is far calmer.

Really, the big difference is that I'm not fixing and searching for answers people didn't ask me to find and then getting angry because they didn't do the thing I told them to do.

Instead, I'm cheering my loved ones on as they make their own good choices and sitting in the suck with them when they figure out what to do when they don't.

On good days, I am 100 percent down with my own advice. On others, my survival instincts kick in, the ones that no longer serve me. I have to dig deep, ask for help, and listen to those I trust to remind me of my core value to empower. It is deeply, deeply uncomfortable.

FENCE LINES

One of my earliest memories surrounds walking the fence line each morning with my grandfather on our thirty-acre recreational farm.

Fences get a bad rap. They are often seen as something to keep "others" out. But in my world, they represent safety for those within. A firm boundary of support for those I love. Those fence line walks taught me that boundaries need regular wellness checks if they are to keep me and my people safe.

In my memory, I'm five. I know this because we took this walk each morning before school. I'd be up and out the door, having stared at the full breakfast of grits, sausage, and eggs my mother put in front of me, and finally being released with her frustrated sigh over the fact that while I'd compliantly sat at the table with her, my father, and my brother, all I'd done was push the food around and drink half a glass of milk. Bless my mother. She was convinced I would starve. She was not aware of, or perhaps not considering, the 3 a.m. chocolate cake I'd consumed with my father that was keeping me alive.

I would be in my "outside" clothes because fence walking will get a girl's school clothes dirty. My grandfather, also known as Pa, would help me pick out a "good" stick, and we'd proceed to walk through the woods and fields that surrounded the property. The fence was nothing more than a low-voltage wire wound on stakes with yellow plastic knobs. And yet, it kept all the dogs, five at the time, on the property, even when it wasn't working. One good shock, and a dog learns quickly to steer clear. The six of us kids were not as quick as the dogs. We shocked ourselves on the regular, testing the boundaries and each other.

The sun would be just over the horizon or not quite there as the winter came on, when we began our adventure. The job was to make sure there was nothing on the fence or amiss on the edges of the property. We would pull off sticks and limbs and other various debris.

It was a peaceful, purposeful way to start the day. A long walk in the woods and fields ensuring that all was well, and the animals were safe. It would be followed by feeding the livestock, which consisted of chickens, turkeys, rabbits, goats, pigs, dogs, and barn cats with their copious kittens. Something small and furry would inevitably wind up in the big pocket of Pa's overalls because "the little fella needs a little extra lovin'," and we would go about the business of a wellness check of the farm.

The peace and purpose of these early mornings is something that I hold on to, something that I put a fence around, and a boundary I keep and check on the regular. And so does the conversation. We, whichever of the six grandchildren showed up at the appointed time, would learn about the world as we worked. It wasn't a steady stream of talk. More like long silences and questions carefully listened to and answered. It was the very definition of a safe space.

And even now that I live in a neighborhood, on a quarter acre with a fenced-in backyard where I can see and hear everything happening at the neighbors' houses that surround mine, walking the fence line is something I hold on to tightly.

Most mornings look like greeting the sun with a cup of coffee on the porch, bundled up under the heater provided by the trusty husband because he knows the importance of this ritual even in the winter months. Mornings look like leashing up my good dog and walking through the neighborhood, on the same 3.5 mile path, doing a wellness check of sorts on the world and my people. Sometimes I have the company of good friends, and we solve the world's problems. Sometimes I have the company of messages from good friends through the miracle of technology, and we are solving the world's problems. Sometimes it's just my dog and me, and *we* are solving the world's problems.

Either way, the problems get brought out into the open in a safe space, and the day starts with peace and purpose. And, I feel my Pa's smile and am tucked into his overall bibs for a little extra lovin'.

DEATHBED GIFTS

My grandmother was an avid visitor of the sick and homebound of her tiny church community. She didn't drive. As soon as I turned sixteen and got my license, it became my privilege to be her driver on these visits. She was not a woman with many rules, but in these circumstances, she was strict in what was expected. If the person you were visiting was suffering and it was too much for you to handle, leave the room. Your place is to "bring ease and joy." Those were her words. What I'd say now after many years of following this advice is, "It's my job to hold space." Same. Same.

So, when I was nineteen and came home from college to find my Pa on his deathbed from rapidly spreading cancer, I held fast to this lesson. Bret, then my boyfriend, took me to my cousin's high school football game so someone would be in the stands cheering and/or for emergencies (it was football after all) while my aunt, uncle, and parents sat with my Pa and Grandma. We came back to the house with buckets of Kentucky Fried Chicken, a rare treat in a house that grows, raises, and cooks its own food. I went in to visit my Pa. His hulking frame was sunken in the bed, and he was in obvious pain.

And he had a smile just for me.

"Hello, Sweetheart! How about a little music?"

"On it. Love you!"

With a smile and a kiss on his papery cheek, I scampered to the living room where the piano that he and I had picked out together over a decade earlier sat. He took me to find that piano one Saturday morning because he wanted to learn to play, and I was the one who had the privilege of teaching him. In high school, I was the pianist for his church, and of course, I'd grown up in his house. I knew what he liked. I started banging out an anthem arrangement of "How Great Thou Art" and then on to his favorite rendition of "In the Garden." I barely noticed Bret in the armchair, holding space, eyes closed, listening. A different kind of music for this Rush fan, but he was there for it.

My brother appeared in the doorway. "Don't stop. It's helping him. And all of them."

And so I played on. When I ran out of anthems, I opened the Baptist hymnal at the beginning and leaned in hard. Every verse of every song. Sometimes singing quietly but mostly just my hands on the keys. Steady and joyful.

I played for hours deep into the night. I don't remember Bret ever moving from his spot. Holding steady, holding me up, having my back.

Around 3 a.m., I stopped. I sat there, hands resting on the keys. The house was silent. I felt an indescribable shift.

My father appeared in the doorway and said, "He's gone."

And my heart cracked wide open.

The rest of that night, the memorial service, the burial, are all a blur. But that night with that music is etched in my memory.

It came back to me when Grandma was in hospice, and I sat by her bed singing from the same hymnal.

It came back when my father-in-law was dying, and I climbed in bed with him at 2 a.m. to help him make a spreadsheet of his affairs.

It came back yet again when my mother-in-law was dying, and we were blasting Elvis and sitting with the kids on the floor at the foot of her bed playing UNO Attack.

Each circumstance was different and the same. Holding space and seeing someone I held in my heart from this life to the next. My grandfather showed me the way by asking for what he needed, and in that moment, I became a death doula for those I love. I cherish the gift of every one of those last moments, hold them tightly in my soul, and wouldn't trade them for anything.

CLAIM YOUR JOY

We were in the oncology urgent care for Sloan Kettering. Dr. Giralt was concerned that the cancer had spread to my mother-in-law's brain, and we were there for an emergency MRI. She was most disgruntled when the sainted Dr. Giralt shared the news that we would be headed to the hospital. We had plans for an Irish pub and a matinee on Broadway, as was our tradition with these monthly appointments in New York City.

You see, we had the whole cancer thing under control. Mom had an oncologist in her hometown of Wappingers Falls that she saw regularly and for treatment, and then once a month, I flew up, and we took the train into the city to see Dr. Giralt at Sloan Kettering. Look him up. He's a big deal. He kept Mom alive for six years with cutting-edge medicine when the initial prognosis was six months.

Mom loved the city and Dr. Giralt, but she despised going to that office with "all those sick people." Rather than bemoan the fact that we had to go, we always made a day of it. Nothing lit the woman up like a good Irish pub and a Broadway show, and I tend to agree.

So you can see why she was ticked off when our plans got hijacked with this "brain tumor nonsense." Off we went to the oncology urgent care with me making all the calls to all the family while staying positive and talking her into actually going while talking my husband back in North Carolina off the ledge. My saving grace was that he had tickets to see the Tar Heels play the Wolfpack in the Dean Dome that night with our kids and one of Mom's nieces. The game was televised and started just about the time we got into a room. I turned it on, and she was thrilled not only to be watching basketball, but also to be looking for her grandchildren, son, and great niece in the crowd.

She settled in while we waited our turn for the MRI, but then she had to go to the restroom. Since we were still in the urgent care portion of the hospital and had not yet been admitted, this meant a jaunt down the halls. The place was packed! Very ill people were on gurneys lining the maze of halls and moaning. It was the stuff of nightmares.

However, the MUSAK was thumping, and as we traipsed through the hall, Mom started to feel the rhythm and shake her groove thang. The absolute best part about it was that in all of her dancing, her gown came untied, and there was her backside for all to see. She could have cared less. She boogied all the way to the potty and back, and we were all better for it. The sick in those halls who witnessed that moment found some healing, and my catastrophizing mind chilled out. Heck, I started dancing with her, and we had applause by the time we made it back to the room.

I miss many things about Mom, but this way of finding joy tops the list. Her joy was infectious, and she could find it anywhere. She was her grandchildren's favorite playmate all the way to the end, and my favorite travel companion because Mom brought the *fun* to wherever and whatever was going down.

Goals.

SITTING IT DOWN

Let it go
Let that shit go
Let it *all* go

As a yoga teacher, this is a thing I'm called to say.
In class, I even have read poems about letting go.

And what if letting it all go is too much of an ask?

I mean, if I let it *all* go, then what? I'm holding the
line on some pretty important items.

I'm not engaging in hyperbole when I say
As a mother, we are talking about life and death.

When the kids were small, *the* job was quite literally
to keep them alive.

Now that they are mostly grown,
the job is to hold the things
The things they don't have the life experience to hold
While getting out of the way while they *get* the
life experience
And at the same time being available when they

need help
Figuring out life.

It's a fine line.

And at the same time, there are things I can toss off
of my beam.

Today I was verklempt
Because an idea for my writing flitted away
before I could jot it down.

I was in the middle of working with a client,
She was sharing the secrets of her soul.
Now that I examine that
it would have been wrong for me to pick up a pen or
start typing.
I was there being trusted to listen to *her* words.
To hold them close.
To honor them.

And yes, those words resonated deeply in my heart
and soul
And yes, I had the hit to write about *that* thing.

Except I didn't leave the breadcrumb (read "follow
my own best advice")
And it was gone. Like smoke in the wind.

That is something I can let go of.

So now, when I cue the swan dive from tadasana to
rag doll
When we all swoop down, arms wide from a standing
posture with straight arms overhead and eyes up
To a forward fold where we hug ourselves,
drop our heads,
Unclench our jaws
Relax the space between our eyebrows

I have stopped saying, "And let it all go."

I say instead, "maybe pick one thing to let go,
Just for a breath.
One thing you might throw off of the beam, for now.
Something to sit down for a moment."

Because, let's face it. We are responsible in reality for
so much
And if we let it all go, it could be a tsunami of pain
and suffering

Maybe, just maybe, I need to say
"Find someone you trust and hand it over
Just for a few breaths
Just long enough to find ease
Just long enough to recalibrate
Just long enough to recharge

And then, trust that someone to hand back the things
You want to deal with

And keep the ones
That do not serve you."

A NEW PRACTICE

I had been practicing at the same yoga studio, a mile from my house, for twenty years. I did my 200 hour teacher-training there. It was home.

When I traveled, I would try other studios, and they left me feeling unfulfilled.

When my daughter went away to college, she couldn't find a studio to match the one where we had practiced together throughout her high school career. The same thing happened to my son.

I completed my 300 hour training through another studio, online, and started to deepen my practice in new ways.

I started teaching at the studio where I practiced and learned a very specific approach. The teaching there lit me up!

And then, after four years of that, something shifted for me.

The studio no longer felt like "home." I started practicing in my actual home more often than I went to the studio. I started having deeper conversations about all the parts of yoga and the accessibility of yoga for all bodies.

The studio had not changed.

I had.

So, I took a deep breath and went to a new studio. So new that they didn't even have their permanent space yet. This is the email I sent after that class . . .

Hi!

I truly loved Devon's 6:30am yesterday! I have been practicing at another studio for twenty years and teaching yoga for four years, and I deepened my practice and learned new things!

GLORIOUS!

Thank you!

The all caps GLORIOUS at the end doesn't even begin to cover it. I was just about to give up yoga altogether. This one class with two other women and one teacher in a warehouse reignited my passion for yoga.

There is nothing wrong or bad about the studio in which I practiced and taught for all of those years. It's amazing. And somehow, someway, while I wasn't looking, I outgrew it!

I messaged my friend Shelley and told her I was switching studios. Her response was, "I know this is a decision you didn't come to lightly."

It was not. It was pretty much an existential crisis. I am deeply loyal, and this move felt disloyal. And I had been looking forward to studio practice less and less each day until I found myself practicing in my bedroom for the entire month of December and subbing out the classes I was to teach in January.

Now I was faced with breaking up with my home studio. How did I let them know how much I had loved and appreciated and deeply benefitted from my work with them and that it was time to move on? Just peacing out seemed wrong.

But adding drama to it didn't feel correct either.

In the end, I sent a simple text to the manager:

> *New Year, New Schedule!*
> *I'm taking myself off of the sub list.*
> *Thanks for everything!*

And that was it.

There was no response. I simply stopped getting text messages.

No drama, no crisis, no gnashing of teeth.

Just a growing and deepening of my practice, thereby my work on myself.

RELEASING ANCHORS

Twenty-five years of marriage
And a Pandemic
Led to ten days with just the two of us
Talking about everything and nothing

In the talking about such things
In the safe space of matrimony
With all the time and space in the world
Anchors fell away

Anchors being the things I was holding onto
Tightly and with all my might
Anchors that were simply
Weighing the two of us down.

Societal Pressure
SPLASH!

Anger at the past
SPLASH!

Bitterness
SPLASH!

Shame
SPLASH!

Each had its own story
And So. Much. Weight.
Residing in the back of the cave of my mind
Where the bears may or may not exist

In the sacred space
Sharing everything and nothing
The lights were on
Facts were checked

And we both left
Lighter
Untethered
Free

THE GIFT IN THE PROBLEM

We were in a season. My mother-in-law was very ill. After battling cancer for six years and losing her husband five years before, and living those years to their fullest and with the most possible joy, the Alzheimer's she had feared her whole adult life, and done everything in her power to hold at bay, was creeping in fast. It was beyond gut wrenching.

Big, hard decisions were having to be negotiated and made. Mom was fortunate. Both of her boys and their wives loved her with unbounded ferocity. All decisions for her care were made as a team, and all were thrilled with the idea of having her live with us. It's a good thing to have a team with whom to think through all of the hard decisions. It is, at the same time, difficult to deal with all of the emotions and different perspectives. We were fighting with a double-edged sword.

Such difficult times bring out an old gremlin for me. I am, you'll remember, your girl in a crisis. I will drive the ten hours or will hop a plane if ten hours is too long. I will get on the phone and shake down doctors to get you what you need in a timely fashion. I will stay all night by your side in the hospital. I will smile and laugh with you when you need a lift, and I will hold you while you cry and rail against the unfairness of it all. I'll even take it when you lose your cool and yell at me because the world has gone to hell in a handbasket, and you need to let it out, and I'm the closest target. I am a rock, taking care of business for as long as it needs taking care of.

But once the crisis is handled, I crash. And the gremlin sits at the site of the crash where I beat myself up. It is perfectionism born of so many things. It's a gremlin I've carried with me since childhood. Ingrained self-destructive gremlins are tough to eradicate. In fact, I beat myself up over the fact that I haven't yet sent this particular gremlin packing as it is *so* very destructive not only to me, but also to those around me. I can only take so much self-loathing before I lash out at the one closest to me. I hear all of the words I am saying to myself about being a failure, a burden, not nearly enough, coming out of the mouth that isn't saying them. The putting of words in this particular mouth is complex. There is only one person in my life whose words truly matter to me. That would be my husband, my true partner in life. He is also the exact person who can be absolutely trusted to never say such words to me. The words that I have assigned to him do not exist. And yet, I hear them, then back myself into a corner, and come out swinging. Because *that's* what we all need in a crisis.

At the height of my mother-in-law's illness, I also launched into becoming a licensed yoga teacher. It was during my training that I began to learn ways to reframe a situation to find the gift. Bret, my husband, had been trying to talk to me about focusing on the "what" rather than the "who" for years, but something in this training made it click for me. I am practicing focusing on the "what" of a problem rather than "who" caused it. And I am having success; as long as the stakes stay low. And this, with my mother-in-law, was high stakes. All. Of. The. Time. The moment I started to settle, my phone would chime with some new crisis.

For example, I took a shower one day. A shower. I had all quelled in my house, no one needed hot water, and I was looking forward to a lengthy, all-inclusive cleansing of body and mind. I stayed in the shower for exactly seventeen minutes. In that time, my mother-in-law's oncologist left a cryptic message, and I had two texts, getting more frantic by the second, from my sister-in-law. My reaction? "What was I thinking, taking a long shower?" The moments I'd set aside for self-care were torn asunder. I jettisoned myself from the shower, hair dripping, wrapped in a towel, and I came out swinging at the overworked nurse in the oncologist's office who was just trying to do her job. I had no chill, no balance, and no self-love or grace was anywhere to be seen.

I have to stop with the self-loathing. Period. Not just when it's little stuff that's going sideways, but *all* of the time and *especially* when it's the big stuff. You see, I can't own the title of "your girl in a crisis" if I'm going to then *cause* a crisis with my self-hate after it's all over.

It's no wonder I wasn't able to catch my breath. I'd been too busy solving one major crisis after another followed by beating myself up for needing to take whatever time needed to recover from dealing with said crisis. There *was* no recovery. Just anxiety and anger and bitterness. And if that's the way it was going to be, all would be better without my help no matter how efficient or useful I was in the moment.

This was the exact opposite of my grandmother's caretaker teachings. Add to that the yoga teachings I was studying, and I found help to see that there is no freedom in self-loathing. All of the yoga teachings speak of living in the moment. Not the past, not the future, just the moment. To do otherwise brings only anxiety and depression. To live in the moment brings joy. Self-loathing over the "who" of a problem is living in the past. Trying to keep something bad from happening is dwelling on a future that we have no way of knowing what will hold.

The gift in the problem (and there is always a gift in a problem I've learned) of the end-of-life decisions we were having to make for my sweet, beloved mother-in-law was the sharp focus that I was getting on the problem of dwelling on "who" rather than "what." It was directly in my face, glaring as *the* issue that is making my life untenable and joyless. It wasn't cancer or Alzheimer's or hospitals or doctors or even death. It was not even the fact that I couldn't seem to take a "real" shower in those days without the whole world exploding. It's all in the way I spoke to myself, the tone I took with me.

And so, I'm vowing to take my grandma's gentle tone with myself. It won't be easy. I can't just will those thoughts away. (I've tried.) But when that gremlin pops up, I'm going to shut that sucker down in the same tone I'd use on a nurse who wasn't taking excellent care of my mother-in-law. It's not unkind, this tone; it simply trucks no nonsense and is not to be argued with. I will tell the gremlin to "have a great day" on its way out the door, and I will mean it. In this way, I will show up for myself, find the magic of self-love, the absolute power that lies there.

WHEN THE MAYO HITS THE FAN
(A STORY OF A FULL MOON)

It was Sunday, which means I was trying to do our food prep for the week. I was throwing ingredients into the food processor for homemade mayo to throw on the eggs I'd already boiled, peeled, and diced to finish off the requested egg salad as my husband walked through the door with the weekly grocery shopping. I reached for the enormous can of olive oil I keep in the cupboard for such recipes (a double batch of mayo requires 2.5 cups of olive oil) and learned that we were out.

How the heck did that happen? I *always* have a metric ton of olive oil on hand.

I shot out a quick text to the girls in the hood expressing my olive oil emergency.

There was no going back to the store. The house rule is to get it during the weekly shopping, or we do without.

I got an immediate answer and took my measuring cup up the street and around the corner.

Olive oil procured, I started the food processor and added the olive oil.

It did not make mayonnaise.

It made olive oil and egg soup.

I don't know why. That's just what happened. And when it did, everything that I'd been holding and carrying came out sideways.

I dumped the mess down the drain and went to our room, closed the doors and cried.

And I mean ugly cried. Gulping, snot, sobbing cried.

Over mayonnaise. Which can be purchased pretty easily at the grocery store. I'm pretty sure they make egg salad too!

But it wasn't the mayonnaise of course, and it wasn't even the fact that I was weary of so very many things. I can handle, well, a metric ton, of things most days. So it wasn't so much that I was holding things in and not sharing what was happening or not asking for help. I had been steadily using my tools. See ugly crying. My tools were not working.

And then, the trusty husband, who keeps up with these things so that I don't have to, informed me that the moon was "not in a forgiving phase."

Well.

And then my friends told me that the moon was full, the Lion's Gate was open, and cosmically, we were in the thick of it.

Now, I'm a fairly practical person who believes in science. (Okay, I do lean witchy if you count the bones in my freezer for broth and the kombucha on my counter.) And I am here to tell you, the moon is a powerful thing. The day Bret and I figured that out and accepted it, things got a *lot* easier around here.

So, armed with this information, I was able to finish my cathartic sobbing and pick up a good book to stop the plates I was spinning in my mind. Of *course* nothing was going right, and the only thing to do was stop hustling so hard and rest.

I ordered takeout and made a plan to buy mayo the next day while I was out running an errand, and we'd be past this moon phase.

I put *all* the things down for the day. They weren't going anywhere.

The moon in her glorious full-ness was forcing me to rest.

Accepting that is truly standing in my power.

BE STILL!

Right here!
This!
This is what acceptance
looks like!

The purposeful
Retreat House
Password.

A play on
WiFi
And the lack of
Stillness available
there.

And yet,
I struggle to
Be Still!
And know
That all is well

To know that
Problems
Are just puzzles

When met
With
Breath,
Intention,
Discussion,
Trust,
Partnership.

In order
To meet them thusly

I must
Be Still!
Stop
"Solving" quickly
In a vacuum.

I must
Be Still
And know
That all is well.

WARRIORS IN HEADSCARVES

I had just dried my parking-lot tears due to the valiant speech Bret had just made about facing whatever happened together as he dropped me off for a breast biopsy and then left to deal with the flooding under the house because of *course*.

I had it together. I found the breast center radiologist office in the maze of the medical center and walked in with calm and head held high.

I was greeted by five women sitting in the waiting room wearing headscarves. And that, friends, is when I lost it. The kind receptionist took one look at me and asked, "Are you looking for the restroom? It's right this way." I nodded, followed directions, locked myself in, and burst into tears. I had not been prepared for that much reality.

After three minutes of sobbing, I pulled it together, put on my warrior face, and headed back out to the waiting room. I stoically checked in, sat down, opened my novel, and lost myself in some excellently written scholarly fiction.

My name was called. I followed all the directions on autopilot, passed out during the post-biopsy mammogram (I mean, why would they *do* that!), gathered my Coke and Cheez-its, and waited calmly for my friend Shelley to pick me up and navigate me home through rush-hour traffic.

I took my Tylenol, kept the ice packs in my bra, and watched *ER* with Bret until bedtime.

I dreamed of those scarves all night.

I woke up shaken. I couldn't get the image out of my mind, and it was making my heart race, which doesn't feel great when your left breast has been biopsied. I was certainly borrowing trouble.

I could hear my grandmother's admonishments about the borrowing of trouble whispered in my ear. I dug deep, and I reframed the experience with some truth. Yes, seeing those scarves was terrifying. And, in reality, I was surrounded by my warrior sisters as I faced down this biopsy and whatever it had to say.

That reframe carried me through the waiting period to see what was what, which turned out to be nothing to worry about. It also reframed doctors' offices in general. We are there to fight. We are warriors together, supporting each other. I've been great at this for a long time when I was not the patient. I look people in the eye, I smile, I offer comfort. Had I lifted my head from my book, I could have received the same.

Lesson learned. Be in the world. Meet myself where I am. Don't be so freaking stoic, and receive.

WALKING THE WALK

"Completely benign. Let me repeat that again for the people in the back. I said, 'Completely benign.'"

This is how my doctor entered the room where Bret and I sat huddled together, back to back ready to fight tooth and nail.

We exhaled. We talked about breast density, family history, and aggressive steps. The long and the short of it is that I do not have breast cancer, *and* I will be having yearly breast MRIs going forward due to the density of my breasts.

And that's not what this essay is about. I just wanted to announce that all is well.

This essay is about walking the walk with my children when it comes to taking care of myself and promises I've made over the years as we've dealt with cancer and the deaths of their grandparents.

"I have some less than awesome news," I said cheerily into the phone as my daughter and son-in-law were chatting with me on a two hour drive. "I found a lump in my left breast. I've had two ultrasounds and two mammograms. The good news is that my lymph

nodes are clear, and we caught it early. I am having
a biopsy tomorrow. The doctor said she's pretty sure
it's cancer."

My stoic daughter, who is her mother's child, said,
"Okay," and my heart cracked with her voice. My son-in-
law, who was a third-year medical student at the time,
went into full caretaker mode. He was holding both of
us. Me with his calm measured tons. Her with his hands.

I answered the questions and then ended the topic
with a "how was your weekend?"

I've had a lot of hard conversations in my life. Many
of them, with my children. Many of them with my
children about cancer and someone they cherish. And
this was the hardest five minutes of my fifty-one years.

I didn't want to say anything until after the biopsy
in case there was nothing to tell. And my daughter had
made me promise not to hold back hard information
years before when her grandparents were sick and dying.
I had already broken our pact the moment I didn't tell
her I had found a lump. (I apologized for that.)

I did not tell my son. He was away at school, his love
was seven hours away, and I wanted to wait until I had
all of the information and could look him in the eye and
wrap my arms around him and reassure him that this
was not that. He and I do not have the same pact, *and* I
would never hide facts from him.

After that phone call, the tears came. The ones that
didn't come when I found the lump or had the tests
or the doctor said "probably cancer." Because I knew
it was going to be okay. A pain in the ass maybe, but
okay nonetheless.

But my children, who have suffered and lost so much to cancer . . . to have to tell them that now their mother probably has it in her body . . . that right there was unbearable.

In that moment, I understood my in-laws. For both of them, we had to pry the information out of them. Both of them waited far too long to tell us anything or even see a doctor, in my opinion. And now I know why. They were not afraid for themselves. They didn't want to hurt their children.

So I find myself walking in their shoes. A real, calm smile on my face and in my voice, agreeing to continue to be aggressive with cancer.

In the end, I didn't have to tell Mason anything because by the time he got home, everything was all clear. However, what I let go of was being the "only" person who can hold and comfort my children. I never knew what a gift it would be for my children to find partners in life until I had to share horrific news about myself. This was beyond hard. It would have been insurmountable without the care of my children's partners.

It turns out that walking the walk that was modeled for me by my amazing in-laws was the act of receiving. In this situation, I had no control over the outcome. While I can choose to be aggressive in my health, cancer is, well, cancer. And in keeping my promises, I was forced to receive.

Uncomfortable.

And when I leaned into it, such an amazing gift.

YOGA AS RECEIVING

I am reminded of waaayyy back, twenty-five years ago, when I started the practice of yoga using Shiva Rae's DVD's, I noted that it felt more like I was healing my body than "working out."

However, as time marched on and I replaced running with yoga, I would habitually turn on my Apple Watch in the hot studio and gleefully record 500+ calories burned in an hour. I talked a lot, and I've written a lot, about that banging practice replacing seven-minute miles.

And, recently, my hip started bothering me again, and my doctor gave me a heck of an athletic workout for physical therapy. It's thirty minutes of strength training every other day. I have a dog who needs to walk two to three miles a day every day. He and I like to walk fast! That right there is a workout regime.

Adding a 500+ calorie-burning yoga practice to that was just, well, too much! And yet, I felt guilty for not practicing in the studio. I was disconnected from my practice and my body.

And then, just like that, three weeks had gone by with no yoga. Life was life-ing and my body was craving the warm embrace of asana but not the heat or the pace or the time commitment of a studio practice.

I reminded myself that I am a 500-hour certified yoga teacher.

I reminded myself that breathing *is* yoga.

I reminded myself that I need to stretch my hips and wrists and shoulders and, well, my whole body, to feel good.

I reminded myself that I "work out" plenty.

I reminded myself that I have created a life of schedule flexibility.

So at 10 a.m. on a Thursday, when people "should" be cleaned up and working, I reminded myself that I'd been "working" since 6:30 a.m. when I returned from walking my good dog, and perhaps it was time for a break.

I threw on some clothes that I could move in, (I was still bundled up from my early morning walk in 27 degree temps), turned on the fire in my bedroom, turned off the lights, and rolled out my mat.

For the first time ever. I mean the first time in twenty-five years of practicing yoga at home, in the studio, and in foreign lands, I left my hair (and I have a lot of it) down. The constriction of a ponytail made me want to cry.

Unusual.

Typically I'm a "messy bun, get it done" kind of gal. However, on this random Thursday, the loose waves falling in my face set the tone for what I was about on my mat.

I had a playlist I'd carefully crafted for a yoga retreat I led under the moniker "Holding on and Letting Go." I put in earbuds to drown out the world and let it play as I settled into child's pose and gave myself permission to stay there until the music stopped.

The beat picked up, and after I finished stretching my wrists, which were like "*Gurl! Where you been!*" I rolled over my feet and lifted my hips for my first downward facing dog.

As I moved slowly and intentionally through poses, quietly humming along with the music that nourished me on a different level with each song, I felt a mind, body, spirit shift. I felt wrapped in a giant hug. And *whew*, did I need it.

I finished and posted this image and caption to the socials. I was promoting nothing and didn't even mention my programs or books. It was a simple public service announcement. A blessing if you will, for all those I could reach.

I had given myself the biggest gift by rolling out my mat and practicing slowly and gently.

Yes . . .

Exhale . . .

My yoga practice has begun to be about acts of self-love. I get plenty of workouts in, and don't get me

See the unmade bed? See the dirty, tangled hair? See the hot mess? See ME!

wrong, strength training and cardio are acts of self-love as well, but this is a different level.

I've been a multitasker pretty much since birth. (I'll have to fact-check that with my mother, but I have a feeling she'd agree.) If I can kill two to four birds with one stone, I'm down. Self-love *and* a workout, two requirements for a strong body and mind, get me moving before 6 a.m. every morning with my good dog. Add the third stone of keeping him happy and balanced. Heck YES! And then my strength training that doubles as physical therapy—friends, I'm the best patient that my physical therapist has!

But this hair-down yoga practice is letting go of the multitask need. In fact, as I write this, I am vowing to take off my Apple Watch that is counting "workout time" as I do this practice. No pony tail, no watch.

Holy Hannah, I'm free in the breeze over here.

And it feels so amazing!

In this practice, I get to practice receiving—my truest growth edge.

EPILOGUE:
THE GIFT OF EMPOWERMENT

"The Field" where I grew up was a recreational farm. Besides walking the fence and caring for animals, my Pa taught me to raise and butcher hogs. As odd as that sounds these days, in doing so, he brought me a deep sense of safety and belief in myself.

You may need to read that line again, take a deep breath, and trust me. My grandfather taught me that I had power in a world where I felt powerless.

Everyone had a job, the way I remember it. The whole process ran like clockwork, and if you had asked me at age eight, it was almost better than Christmas. Hog-butchering weekend lives in my memory devoid of all of the fear and anxiety I felt as a child.

In my mind it was magical.

As an adult, I know my grandfather was the waver of that wand. Looking back on these weekends now, I recognized that he built this ritual around all of us as a bonding activity and as a way of creating a sense of safety.

You see now, I joke (sort of) with friends about being your girl in the zombie apocalypse because I know I could call up those deeply ingrained food raising and butchering skills should the need arise. There is comfort in that for my catastrophizing brain. And at the end of the day, am I really that far off?

We have just lived through a global pandemic. Feeling secure in one's ability to put food on the table is the stuff we watch the folks in Alaska do on TV. I have those skills, buried deep, because my grandfather taught us.

He didn't have to. We lived a life of privilege. Grocery stores were plentiful. He owned a lucrative car parts business. He drove a Mercedes to church.

He taught us to raise and butcher hogs purely for the sake of passing down that sense of safety in knowing one can provide for oneself should the need arise. As a child, Pa had not enjoyed privilege, and he knew the value of a hand up, in his case, offered by a man who owned a bakery and gave him a place to sleep and a job when he found himself homeless and alone at thirteen-years-old.

He built everything he built to protect his children and grandchildren from ever experiencing what he had. He was *our* hand up. He would not have used the word "empowerment," but that's what he taught me and what I aspire to carry over into my own work and with my own family.

Empowerment is what allows a girl to "safely" release the outcome.

It's a trusting in one's self to make the next correct choice and go from there.

It went like this. The men would pick a date, a process that usually began with my grandfather exclaiming, "Boys, I think we're gonna have some pig killin' weather this weekend!"

This simple phrase would start the gears turning. He still spoke to his sons with a father's authority, though they were both grown with families of their own. Affecting wisdom beyond my years, I'd tell all of my friends at school, "It's pig killin' weather." The statement always drew very strange looks because I felt like I was the only kid in my large suburban school district who even had a clue what that meant (or where pork chops came from).

As a part of the preparation for the big event, my brother would split extra firewood all week. His job was to be sure that there was enough to keep the water in giant cast-iron pots going all night for various parts of processing the pigs. My grandfather would continue to feed the pigs each morning, talking to them, scratching them with a stick, just like it was any other day. It never occurred to me, as I sat on the designated bucket watching (a ritual that began when I fell into the slop trough in my new Easter dress one spring) to warn the pigs that they would soon adorn our table and fill our meat house with their parts. I was a farm girl, and these things were just a part of nature.

Friday would finally come, and I would be so excited that I could barely pay attention to my teacher's instructions on writing in cursive. On the playground, I told my friends who listened in awe or fear about the whole process. To them, it was something out of a slasher movie. To me, it was a trip back in history to the frontier days. Even at eight, I knew that when the sun set that night, my family would go through a ritual stolen from another time. We would go with my grandfather back to his childhood in Johnston County. In my mind, we would become a delightful combination of the Waltons and the Ingalls family, minus all of the tears.

It didn't seem to matter to my grandfather that he could buy fresh meat from his pig farmer cousins who still lived down east. As a matter of fact, to him this farm in the city was a chance to recreate the good parts of his childhood and erase the bad. My grandfather had money, plenty of it, for which he and his sons had worked hard. There had been lean times in tiny houses nestled on one-acre plots. Some men buy expensive cars and Italian suits when they finally make it big. My grandfather bought another kind of dream: a farm on which he could raise enough food to feed an army for the winter without worrying about what would happen if it failed.

Finally, the bell would signal our release from school, and my brother and I, once home, would run to the barn to check the firewood one more time. The time between 3:30 p.m. and 6:30 p.m., crawled because at this magical hour, the daddies and my grandfather would return from the world of car parts and business and the transformation would begin.

As soon as we saw my father's truck come through the arches that marked the entrance into "The Field," my heart would pound straight out of my chest. There was no need to ask the usual question—"What are we going to do tonight, Daddy?"—because we knew the answer. Jumping into the back of the truck, we hitched a ride back to the house where I would take Daddy's coat, and Johnny would take his hat and carefully put them in the closet for the time when he would have to return to the real world. Lighting a cigar, he would kiss my mother, pat her rump, and say, "Bird Dog, Bo, you better get dressed, the temperature's droppin'!"

That was all I needed to hear. I would run to my room and carefully assemble my pig-killing ensemble. First, I had to pull on my special long johns. Next came my thick wool socks, twelve sizes too big because they were my brother's out-grown hunting socks, only to be worn on pig-killing days and in snow storms—extenuating circumstances when I would become "a boy" despite the pink roses on my long underwear. Next, my pig-killing britches, a pair of handed-down, faded denim overalls. Now that they've become trendy, I can't walk past someone wearing overalls without smelling the hickory fire and our barnyard.

Finishing the inner layer, I would pull on my tan Ocracoke sweatshirt from one of my grandparents' adventures at the beach and run to the mudroom to have my mama fasten the straps on my overalls. By the time I'd made it to this point, Daddy would have taken his shiny pistol from its special place and would be gone to the barn. My brother would be moving *very* slowly getting his pig-killing attire together, and Mama would be digging through the hat and glove box trying to see what gloves and hats would fit us this year.

My brother and I would take our time, putting on coats, mittens, and brogans because though he was an avid hunter, and I was accepting of what would happen, neither one of us wanted to be present for the shots that would end the lives of the pigs. As a matter of fact, things started to fall apart the year we *were* present.

Standing by the back door, staring at the brown pebble linoleum, we would wait to hear the guns ring out, lacing our shoes just right, and nervously chattering like we weren't stalling.

Finally, POW, POW, POW.

"WHEW HAAAA!"

"Good shot!"

The signal that the dirty work was done, and the pigs were no longer the living, breathing creatures that snorted and grunted and nuzzled your hand. We would look at each other and say, "Here we go." And we were out the back door and across the yard to the barn faster than my mother could say, "Now keep your hats on and don't fall in the fire!"

My memories of the next few hours of the ritual are filled with odd details. By the time my father or my uncle drug the pig out, the blood would be only a large dark spot in the mud of the pig pen, and the pig itself would have only a tiny trickle of blood on its mouth and throat like it had gotten tangled up in the briars. The pig would be rolled into the trough now filled with boiling water, thanks to my brother's firewood. It would be rolled a couple of times, and then my grandfather would test the fur. If he could easily pull it out, the pig would be lifted by its feet to the ground where my uncle, my father, and my grandfather would quickly scrape the pig with the special scrapers that looked like discs on a handle before the skin cooled down.

My grandmother would appear from nowhere at some point with a yellow dishpan to collect the liver, a huge red thing. She would go back to the house, and the butchering would begin. A huge table and space heaters would be set up inside the barn, and my mother, the butcher's daughter, would direct the making of pork chops, hams, and sausage meat. A couple of hours would fly by in a whirlwind of activity, and by that time, I would be getting terribly sleepy, and though I'd struggle to stay awake and see the show, I would fall asleep in a hay bale next to the heater.

I would inevitably wake up to Daddy scooping me into his arms as he carried me out of the barn. I would smell the pig cooking in the pit, becoming barbeque. My grandfather and uncle would be dark forms sitting over the hole in the ground, their faces illuminated by the embers. "Good Night, Sweetheart, see you at breakfast," my grandfather would drawl as Daddy walked me up to sleep in the "girl's room" at Grandma's. Snuggling in the double bed next to my sleeping cousin, I would be too tired to be jealous that my brother would get to stay at the barn all night with the men.

"RISE AND SHINE," my grandfather's voice would boom through the house! Up I would pop, dressing and running into my grandmother's huge dining room for a breakfast of eggs, grits, biscuits, and fresh pork tenderloin. The butter and cheese would melt into each homemade biscuit and drip down my fingers as I stuffed the tender meat into my mouth, tasting all that much better because my grandfather was telling me that it was all that corn I fed those pigs from my hands that made it so good. "Good enough to take first prize in any fair," he would say.

The rest of the day would be filled with grinding sausage in the barn, the grinder perched on the back of the pick-up, me sitting on the back of it to keep it balanced. The squiggly pieces of meat would pour from the little holes into the yellow pans one right after another. I would spend the afternoon making sausage patties and helping my mother wrap them to freeze.

At the end of the day, we would tour the full freezers and meat house stocked with chops, hams, sausage, and barbeque, feeling successful and proud that come what may, we would have food for the winter, and we had done it all ourselves. A feeling that most little Charlotte girls never experienced or even knew they needed to.

What I remember most about those weekends is the feeling of togetherness and invincibility my family had. I felt safe and special. I knew that it was something rare. When I was eight, I knew that we were a true pioneer family. If I could hold on to that feeling throughout the rest of the year, everything crazy that was happening around me would be okay.

The last time we butchered pigs was the winter of my senior year of high school, and the magic somehow ceased to exist. It had been years since we had raised hogs, and one of my cousins had begged my uncle and my grandfather all summer, "Let's get some more pigs." My grandfather wanted another chance to teach someone the old ways and accepted. I think he already knew that my uncle and father would not carry on the tradition in his absence and hoped that my cousin would.

The first glitch came with trying to find a cold weekend in January when everyone could be there. Older and multiple kids mean full weekends in any family. Six kids meant absolute craziness in terms of scheduling.

That year, I saw the shot that killed the pigs. My uncle and father had to rig a pulley system to get the pigs in and out of the vat, and my mother complained of the cold, the work, and missing her Friday night date with my father. The sausage seasoning was bad, and later the power went out, and the meat in the freezer spoiled. At least the huge hams my grandfather salted down and put in the meat house survived.

Two years later, my grandfather was dead. Cancer took him from us, and family weekends like these ceased to exist. Oh, we still got together occasionally, but things just weren't the same. "It's hard to get fifteen people together now that they have their own lives and their own families." That's the excuse we used. The old ways didn't seem nearly as important to everyone.

As far as pigs went, no one wanted to chase them when they got out of the lot, no easy task I might add, or take the time to feed them and care for them. We could easily buy the meat at the store.

Now, at Christmas, we get our hams from Harris Teeter. It just doesn't taste the same. I guess no one feeds those pigs corn out of her hand.

In my mind, the yellow shed still sits in the pig lot by the barn. I have to admit, I haven't dared to look in over a decade. The lot's electric fence is no longer active though the one around The Field is stronger. We haven't killed a pig since my grandfather died almost thirty years ago. As a matter of fact, we haven't been the same family since he died. I think this is due to a combination of factors: growing up, growing old, growing apart, moving on. All of those bring a change to families. Maybe it was just coincidence, or good fortune for my grandfather, that things started to change only after he left us. Maybe we were left with the memories of the good ol' days, his presence being a part of that, for a reason. Maybe a solid foundation for us kids to build our lives on. An untarnished image of this man we loved and idolized. Maybe we would have lost that magic if he had lived longer as we grew older and came to understand more of the realities we were dealing with.

It's a strange thing, but the gift of abilities handed down by my grandfather and the knowledge that I possess them if needed have seen me through some of my darkest times. Somehow, it is a talisman, reminding me that I am a survivor.

It is empowerment.

His words about the meat tasting so good because I fed the pigs from my hand reminds me to be grateful for the meat on my table and cognizant of how it was farmed. It reminds me to practice integrity not only in what I eat, but also in how I go about getting it. I loved those pigs with all of my little girl heart. It was my privilege to talk to them and care for them each day with my grandfather. And knowing in my soul that I, in my own way, had put that good food on the table gave me power when I was feeling powerless.

It is receiving.

Everyone had a role in the hog-butchering event. We were a team, each person operating in their zone of genius. Each receiving the help of others to literally put food on the table, to meet a basic need. There is power in that receiving.

As I've read through these essays and thought about the journey on which I'm taking you, the reader, it hit me. I am a caretaker and a nurturer. I have been since I was a child. I am happy to help just about anyone, anytime. And, when I had that breast cancer scare, I had to come face to face with asking for real, deep help, not only from my fantastic support network, but also from my children, whom I learned were actually a part of that network. I was forced to lean on kind doctors and nurses and knowing eyes of strangers in the waiting room.

It was *hard*.

Your girl in a crisis was having her own crisis.

As I read these essays and thought about what my message might be, it is to receive. Nurturing is my superpower. It's also a survival mechanism that does not always serve me and sometimes has me borrowing trouble.

If I want to empower those around me, I need to allow myself to be nurtured as well. I need to reach back to those lessons my Pa was teaching, every so quietly, about partnering and teamwork.

That right there, being open to receive, is my current work. It's knowing that, sometimes, I must put it *all* down. I must receive. Putting it all down and letting someone else pick it up is the ultimate act of releasing the outcome. And in so doing, I offer the greatest lesson I can teach by modeling it. Because we all know, it's in the doing, not the saying.

ACKNOWLEDGMENTS

As one does when one completes a book, I've been rolling around all the names of those I want to be sure to thank for the hand up in the writing of this particular work.

I will begin with Dr. Sam Watson. He strolled into the Expository Writing course I was required to take for my master's in English education in the fall of 1999 and changed my world. With his "Grisley Adams" hair and beard and ever-present cup of coffee balanced precariously on his knee, he managed to convince me that not only was I a gifted storyteller, but also the "essay" was much more exciting and complex than the five-paragraph things I had been churning out in my academic career up to that point. The bulk of the essay that ends this book, "The Gift of Empowerment," was my final project for his class. (It had a different title, but that is long lost.) I guess I got an A, but I honestly don't remember, which is a big deal for the recovering grade grubber. What I remember is the way I felt turning that stack of pages in (because in 1999 papers were turned in printed and stapled). I felt like a writer. I was thrilled and excited by my words. I knew in my bones that this story belonged in the world someplace, sometime.

Which brings me to the next group I want to thank, composed of all (and there are many) the people who said that this final essay most decidedly did not belong anywhere else I've ever tried to put it. Over the course of the books I have published, this essay has appeared many times, and many times, friends, beta readers, and editors have said, "Not here. Not now." They were absolutely correct. This essay has been waiting for this book, and I want to thank this book's beta readers, Lacy, Kelli, and Jeanie, for affirming that now is the time.

To my children, who have raised me as Bret and I have raised them. You challenge me to be better every day and taught me to live in the land of curiosity and figuring it out as we go.

To Shana, my business partner and friend, who could see this book when I could not and coached me off the ledge on numerous occasions during the writing of it. May all writers have such a truth-telling, empowering coach with whom to work.

To the Synergy Publishing Group team for herding this particular cat and making the magic of book production happen by reminding me that I'm even writing a book in the first place, editing, proofing, and creating the gorgeous artwork through what could only be considered mind reading. Ya'll are truly magical.

To Bret, who has loved this last essay from the moment I wrote it and been willing to read it over and over through the years as I've put it in front of him again and again asking for his thoughts.

And to my Pa for the "little extra lovin'" he always had at the ready for me.

ABOUT THE AUTHOR

Cindy is a wife and mom who loves cooking wholesome food, reading good books, traveling, and being in the woods or near the water with her husband and children. A former high school teacher and university professor, Cindy is now the founding partner of Synergy House LLC (where she loves to host retreats and feed people) and the managing partner of Synergy Wellness Group. As a part of this work, she is the lead writing coach for Synergy Publishing Group, an ICF certified, BodyMind Method© coach, and an RYT 500 yoga instructor.

Each of these roles tap into her super power of helping people reclaim themselves (or maybe claim themselves for the first time), teaching small group yoga, and talking to groups of all sizes and demographics about her books, her writing, and the messy process of writing. Her current focus is on getting as many voices out into the world as possible because people's stories matter and the telling of those stories is healing. In this way the claiming, the yoga, and the writing all come together for her. And sometimes she even follows her own best advice.

Learn more about Cindy and her work
by connecting on Instagram
@cindy_d_urbanski
@synergywellnessgroup

You can schedule a chat at **thesynergywellnessgroup.com.**